Introduction

This small novel collection is a source of inspiration for me and for my surroundings, close friends and family. Though light to read, this series of tiny novels open up a whole understanding of the animal's elaborate consciousness process, and show how sophisticated their communication can be, as we can only suspect it to be...

For this of course is simply based on assumptions and has absolutely no scientific proofing ambition, of course. Validating it through experimentation would prove very difficult. Though, the events are explained down to the facts, and related to what seems to be the actual outcome of the situations that have been encountered.

Some of those stories were told to a national park guard on deviant Art, and acknowledged into their insight and realness. I have included a comment of this sympathetic contact to make the story more alive and real!

Those stories are brought partially from comments written on deviant Art, but have been partially reformulated in order to correct them and make them addressable to a wider audience. Only corrections in the form have been performed. The stories themselves, of course, remain as experienced.

We hope you'll have as much fun to read that I had encountering those situations: have a good read!

1. The Crows and my Cottage's chimney

I used to have a nice old cottage in the Belgian countryside near the seaside of Knokke, in the polders countryside. Land that was taken over the sea: I remember finding shells in the ground of the cottage's garden when I was a small kid, as the seashore was several kilometers away, not to be seen: only agricultural fields surrounding the area and a cow field as well.

On that cottage, while I was living alone in it, there was an open chimney for the chimney closure system was quite rusted it stayed open. One day I noticed after being absent that crows had actually penetrated in the house through the chimney, and two were trapped in the house when I came back at the end of the week..

Let me explain you how this story unveiled...

Its quite strange to come back home and notice crows buzzing on the windows like large black flies, I can tell you it tames your energy, plus there was a lot of decoration in the house so I had to act very careful to grab them also not to hurt them. Which I succeeded.

The next week, There was one crow alive and one crow dead, dehydrated, again, they penetrated in, through the chimney. The dead one didn't find anything to drink in the house while the last time there was a cooking pan full of water in the kitchen (I was absent during the week and came to the cottage during the weekend then). I released the one that had stayed, and started wondering how to solve the problem, of these crows entering the cottage by the chimney.

The next day, I was in the house, and one crow stared at me all puzzled right from into the chimney! Then he exited it.

There was a large painting representing the cottage with a large sky, and the crow stared at it in full panic, and then started to fly at it and tried escaping through that part of the painting that represented the sky! Wrong luck!! (He banged his head on it trying to get through it to fly in the sky).

Anyway, taking the opportunity at the little stunned crow, I captured him and went with him in the garden. Only I didn't let him go just yet.

I started talking to him. He of course was all excited, and as you know crows always try to bite at your fingers and all, and he was no exception. Once calmed down, I started talking to him as imaged I could: "This is the house, going into the house dangerous, you can die if you go into the house, no drinking", and so on. Very simple language. It looked like he was listening to me with great attention!

I decided he was ready so I released him. He flew directly to a large tree area in the next-door farm where crows usually gather, which is what happened then: a large gathering of crows occurred there.

Then followed some great commotion! You could hear them crow for at least 15 min, and after that, no single crow ever tried to go back into the chimney (which remained open)!

I figured out that for them they were so curious that they were collecting 'amazing' info from the survivors of the chimney trip that must be part of crow-mystics now!

SlowDog 294: "Wow. You possess a rare skill: animal kinship. This is a definite park ranger trait.

Awesome story, my brother. I believe you were right about the crows passing on knowledge of your encounter with them in the house. The thing about birds is how efficient their high speed dialogue is.

A bird can say more with one chirp than humans can within a very thick book. To an average human, they all sound the same. However, to a perceptive pair of ears such as yours, the conversation is all too transparent. Very profound, indeed."

2. Lausanne's Starlings on the Tree

Birds can have amazing communication skills. Some of them who are operating in large groups especially, have impressive skills, which we can only guess at how far they operate.

About the communication speed, when I was studying in Switzerland at EPFL (Polytechnic Lausanne), once during late spring there were a couple of starlings that landed on a tree located behind the sofa window..

I was in a special state of mind at the time and I soon realized how efficient their communication was: not only was I able to have a clue at what they were exchanging, but also I could have a clue about more details of their exchange; it was extremely quick and the language, very accurate on the environment that they describe.

It made me think about the instructions air force fighter pilot exchange on the radio (I'm a big fan of aeronautics since my early childhood), though quite more poetic as of the quality of what they were in the process of describing.

We also have a lot of blackbirds in Belgium, and these, I really enjoy listening to their sunset songs: they always have short beautiful phrases that describes elements of the day, it's like the news at sunset, nature version.

They're truly amazing. Morphologically close from mynas - they are able to learn to speak I suspect, if they have 'the' education that allows to do so.

It's only when I was living in Switzerland that some of that type of nature became available, because of residing in small countries like Belgium, Switzerland or Israel you of course never have as large stretches of nature.

It's awesome and I wish I could visit and experience proper interaction with rangers one day, in an area where nature at large is explorable.

3. The Falcon morning fuzz

It was a morning, relatively early on, and I was sleeping tight after a busy evening the day before. I was in my cottage at the seaside in Belgium, located in the countryside of Knokke, near the North Sea.

Suddenly I was woken up by an unusual rumble outside in the garden. I was sleeping in an under-the-roof apartment on the top level of the cottage.

All of the windows in my room were shut with shades; so in order to get to see quicker what was happening outside, I stepped out of my room and in the hallway, where there was a large velux type of window, on the roof, that I could look through.

I decided to open it, in order to better perceive what was going on. At first, still sleepy, I noticed about nothing.

But then, the sounds came back and I was very suprized to witness a hawk pursued by a whole bunch of crows! The falcon was flying fast, in the first position, and a delta shaped cloud of crows was after him/her..

It is then that I decided to actually do something about the situation... I suddenly started to make a whole lot of noise and fuzz by myself, right when the crows came back at my height!

Scared (they are wild in the area around my cottage), they started to disperse, and the fuzz was suddenly over...

Appalled by my success, I started looking around, left, right, and nothing was to be seen anymore.

I was about to start my day and to close the velux window located on the roof... That is when, for some reason, I felt observed, and looked on top of me, though the velux, still open (it was horizontal)...

There was the falcon, in stationary flight, looking at me. That was quite an incredible feat, because normally the falcon was afraid of me and of any humans living in the vicinity, as across several hundred meters, there was just one neighboring farm around, then nothing but the next farm, probably 200 or 300m away...

That was it, and I could continue my day.

But the next days and for some time afterwards, I noticed that the falcon was observing me, and as a show of gratitude, was flying next to my car when I was driving on our street in the countryside, which, considering the fact that it was a wild falcon, he realized I was in the car and that he was greeting me by following my car, figuring out I was inside driving it!

Nature really can truly be amazing!

4. The Crow's magic ball at the Zwin

The Zwin is a nature reserve at the seaside of Belgium, at the North Sea. There used to be a theme park in the Zwin, where many bird cages and different endemic (local) and other birds to be seen.

Fortunately, now the cages are all gone, and the town mare has forbidden to lock birds into cages.

Among the cages was a very special large crow, who became my friend!

At that time, I used to visit the Zwin's park relatively often, and each time, I stopped by at the big crow's cage, and started greeting him with sounds and talking to him.

He then usually came next to the place I was standing at next to his cage, resting against the fence, which made it possible to gently caress him.

But doing so was not without risks, because this facetious bird had a way of himself, as, after some time cuddling, he was suddenly turning against you and trying to catch your finger with his very large black beak! No-go to have a finger in there, really!

That is when I found a new way to interact with him..

Not very far from where his cage was, there was a countryside cafe with a terrace, and on the terrace was one of these bubble gum dispensers, that also dispensed.. "magic balls", rubber balls that have the specificity of rebounding very high on hard surfaces.

That is the time when I decided to make a little experiment of my own, to buy one of the larger rubber balls (one he could not swallow), and to offer it to him! My plan turned out to be a success! The crow took the ball on his beak, and observed it with a lot of interest!

He did so, until he found a way to go with the present! He went back in the middle of his cage, and started digging a hole to save his precious new gift!

5. The Ducks mating along the street

It was a sunny day of spring and nothing could have prepared me to what I was about to experience...

Everything seemed to be normal around my cottage at the seaside. I wanted to start to drive around to the city to do some shopping, but on the way I noticed something completely abnormal.

It was the ducks' mating season. I don't know what went through their mind, but completely savage ducks were parading on the very edge of the small countryside street, by couples... It was a scene very difficult to explain.

Especially at those locations, the road was very narrow, and could only allow one car through.

There were places where the farmers were riding their tractors to get on to their fields that were usable to cross when 2 cars were presenting themselves face-to-face, and alleys to the farms, so the practice was to use them so that both cars were crossing while having half of their wheel on the side grass, being careful not to dip in the waterways that were present to drain water on both sides of the street.

At several places, inexplicably, they were there, at the very edge of the street, by couples, male and female. They seemed not to be afraid of cars at all.

Of course it was a dangerous situation to them, and I did not know what to do to prevent them to be injured if a car would drive too close to them.

Apparently one couple suffered a loss that way already; the road had many turns up to the small city where the fields ended, and there were almost one couple per street turn.

I only witnessed this once, it never happened again afterwards, to my knowledge.

6. The Story of Smoking Duck

Smoking Duck is the name of a short movie that I directed, that aimed at picturing the effect that weed could have on ducks. My dad had a couple of ducks in his small garden at his house, and they were quacking there pretty happily.

I wasn't living at my father's place anymore, but my eldest younger brother was still living there, it was before he (and I) went to study in Switzerland at the EPFL (the Polytechnic Faculties); I was there with one aim, to use my new hybrid laptop computer...

We completely improvised what was about to follow...

My hybrid laptop was a Sony GT1, a video-camera / laptop hybrid, where a handy-cam lens was integrated on the side of the portable computer, making it either a pretty decent filming unit or a casual, though very small laptop computer.

We watched the ducks, and had an idea. My brother grabbed the male, and started to generate (I was impressed at what he actually produced!) a huge cloud of weed smoke, that engulfed the male duck head and upper body for about 10 full seconds! Amazing sight..

I was filming all along, with the female in the background, a little worried at what the outcome of the experience would be!

It comes out that, while the cloud started to dissipate, the head of the male duck appeared again on the frame, and he quacked pretty loudly, but not worried so much at all; the only thing was that he puffed out a considerable amount of smoke doing so, almost producing a smoke circle...

Considerably amused by that, my brother started to laugh, and could not stop... So I told him to go inside of his room, that offered a direct view on the duck couple, and from there, we tried to witness what the ducks would be doing afterwards...

Well, nothing short of remarkable.. It was quite a surprise, for they first gathered in ordinance side by side, and started very consciously to wash their body feathers... They were very concentrated and in full application on it.

Then, they... started entering a seduction dance, we were quite impressed; and then they started... covering the act!

I finished editing the short movie that was a wintertime postcard.. It became such a success on CKY Forums on the internet... from the Jackass franchise to my dad's garden! Quack!

(No ducks were hurt in the course of this story).

7. The Jerusalem BulBuls' Bart de Wever's message

This one is a little trickier to explain, but I'll try my best!

It is happening at a time when I wanted at all costs to stay and live in Jerusalem, Israel, and I had life restrictions due to my bipolarity, as then I was untreated: my lawyer tried desperately to get me back to Belgium, so I had a very though budget restriction that I had to manage to live with... $600 a month. In Jerusalem.

Try to figure that out!

I had in the end found a solution, for I was volunteering on various projects at the time; that was to use a nearby park in Moshavat Germanit neighborhood in the quieter part of the city, much like a suburban area, and there to settle a "camp". There I planted an Israeli flag to mark my "property".

It was quite magic to live there, because that park is a landscape park where people can come and organize barbecues, in family or in groups, and sometimes people come and plant their tents on it.

I was lucky to have found a quieter area where almost no one was endeavoring, a tree at the edge of a little artificial cliff, where I assembled some kind of Marsupilami nest, extremely comfy inside, and very hidden outside, I tried to make it look as natural as possible.

To decorate the outside, around the camp, I had a few contraptions to retain water, such as a microwave glass plate (that could retain a very shallow pool of water, ideal for the birds), and a bowl of water in it's middle, that I was each day filling with fresh water so that the birds could come and wash themselves every morning, which they happily did.

The bulbul is an endemic species to the region, a middle sized park bird, black and yellow.

For some reason that really stroke my mind, there was one who apparently had learned to master the art of human language, and more strangely he was actually signing and saying a few words in French!

It was so amazing to me, that I recorded his performance, in order to have a proof!

He said it like he had some level of Flemish accent in his French, and he said "petit bourgeois", if you asked me to described his way of saying it, I would say he sounded exactly like the maire of Antwerp, Bart de Wever, in Belgium, a notorious extreme-right politician from the NvA party.

Don't ask me why or how: I have no idea! But that is how he actually sounded! Very specific!!

Conclusion

During the happening of these stories, many things happened. During the story with the great crow, I went back to the place and started to film him – for a documentary pilot I'm working on, about animal consciousness levels – to have some proof of what I was advancing... My sound engineer, Donia, Iranian, was quite appalled by what we were able to bring back on that day... We could film me, caressing the crow, him feeding back with some sweet crowin' and also to try and catch my finger!

I think it is important to put these kind of stories on the table, because I believe in the evolution of animals, through their behavior. I believe that how they can show and differentiate themselves in front of humans can only bring respect to them, and more awareness to the preciosity that their lives represent to us, the value to be able to raise our children witnessing a vivid biodiversity and to be able to have enriching interactions with animals, while respecting wildlife.

Also, knowing how we sometimes perpetrate onto their territories and have them forced to moved, I have to cite a book that I read when I was a small kid. It was for me a great best seller: "The Animals of Farthing Wood". It has been produced as an animation series, from 1993 to 1995. In French it is called "Les Animaux du Bois de Quat'Sous". It is the story of a group of animals that was living in a small wood, that came to be displaced because of a construction project.

As well as in Poltergeist, as in the Hedge, the questions comes back continuously: how do we manage our footprint on this planet, and how can we remain conscious consumers and citizens, respecting our fellows animals, that, after all, are nature's (G-d's) creation, just as we are. Just common sense, to the wider sense.